# FIESTA!

# GERMANY

GROLIER
EDUCATIONAL

Published for Grolier Educational
Sherman Turnpike, Danbury, Connecticut
by Marshall Cavendish Books
an imprint of Times Media Pte Ltd
Times Centre, 1 New Industrial Road, Singapore 536196
Tel: (65) 2848844 Fax: (65) 2854871
Email: te@corp.tpl.com.sg
World Wide Web:
http://www.timesone.com.sg/te

Set ISBN: 0-7172-9099-9
Volume ISBN: 0-7172-9109-X

**Library of Congress Cataloging-in-Publication Data**
Germany.
p.cm. -- (Fiesta!)
Includes bibliographical references and index.
Summary: Describes the festivals of this European country showing how the celebrations with their songs,
foods, and activities express the customs and beliefs of the people.
ISBN 0-7172-9109-X
1. Germany -- Juvenile literature. [1. Festivals -- Germany. 2. Holidays -- Germany.
3. Germany -- Social life and customs.]
I. Series: Fiesta! (Danbury, Conn.)
DD17.G473  1997
943--DC21
97-15219
CIP
AC

*Marshall Cavendish Books Editorial Staff*
Editorial Director: Ellen Dupont
Series Designer: Joyce Mason
Crafts devised and created by Susan Moxley
Music arrangements by Harry Boteler
Photographs by Bruce Mackie
Subeditors: Susan Janes, Judy Fovargue
Production: Craig Chubb

*For this volume*
Editor: Tessa Paul
Writer: Tim Cooke
Designer: Trevor Vertigan
Consultant: Annette Cheyne
Editorial Assistant: Lorien Kite

Printed in Italy

Adult supervision advised for all crafts and recipes
particularly those involving sharp instruments and heat.

# CONTENTS

# GERMANY:

*For about 45 years until 1990 Germany was split into two. Communists governed the eastern part. The country is now united.*

**North Sea**

**Netherlands**

Cologne

Bonn

Rhine

**Belgium**

▶ **Christianity** has played a big part in German history. The Protestant revolt against the Catholic Church began there in the 1500s.

**Luxembourg**

**France**

Rhine

◀ **Berlin** is the capital of Germany. The Brandenburg Gate is a landmark. It stands close to the wall that used to divide Communist East Berlin from West Berlin.

4

**Switzerland**

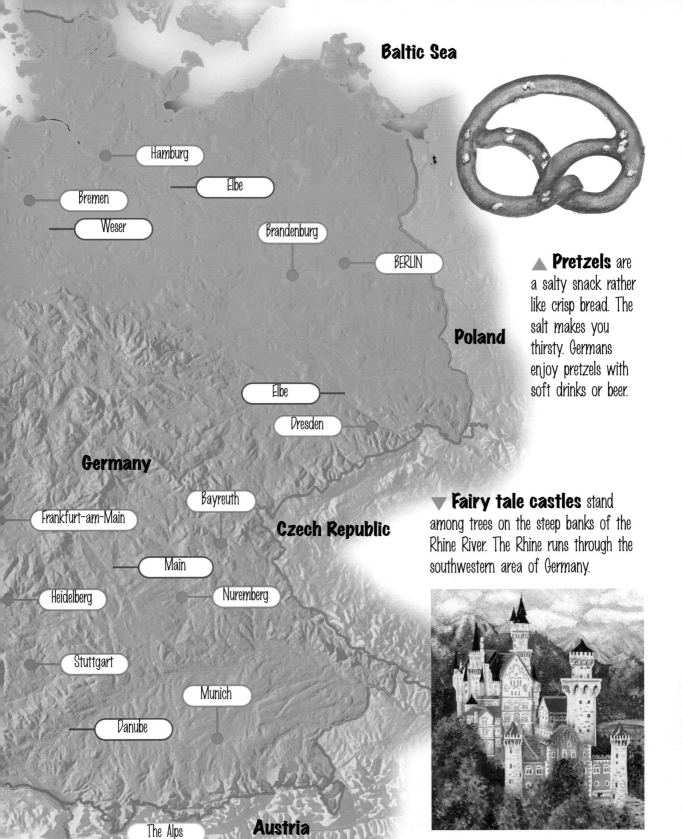

Baltic Sea

Hamburg

Elbe

Bremen

Weser

Brandenburg

BERLIN

Poland

**Pretzels** are a salty snack rather like crisp bread. The salt makes you thirsty. Germans enjoy pretzels with soft drinks or beer.

Elbe

Dresden

Germany

Bayreuth

Frankfurt-am-Main

Czech Republic

Main

Heidelberg

Nuremberg

Stuttgart

Munich

Danube

The Alps

Austria

**Fairy tale castles** stand among trees on the steep banks of the Rhine River. The Rhine runs through the southwestern area of Germany.

# RELIGIONS

*Most Germans are Christians. Around 450 years ago Germany was home to a movement that created a new branch of the Christian faith.*

Germans belong to one of two different churches. Some are Roman Catholics. Others follow the Protestant church, which was born in Germany itself.

In 1517 a German scholar named Martin Luther began to protest about the Catholic church. He did not believe that people should be able to buy themselves the blessing of the church with money or with good deeds. He thought that everyone should have their own relationship with God, without priests to guide them. He did not believe that

*This fiery cross represents the quarrel that divided the Christian church in the sixteenth century. The revolt against the priests was led by Martin Luther.*

church ministers were better Christians than other people.

Luther was thrown out of the Catholic church. But many other Germans shared his beliefs, and gradually they formed their own religion. Because the religion began as a protest against Catholicism, it was called Protestantism. Martin Luther's own particular teachings became known as Lutheranism.

Protestants believed many of the same things the Catholics did. Many of their festivals remained the same.

But in general the Protestants liked religion to be more simple than the elaborate Catholic ceremonies. They did not have images or statues in their churches but did keep the altar and the cross. They thought that all Christians could choose their own best way to worship. The ministers in Protestant sects marry, unlike the priests of the Roman Catholic Church.

# GREETINGS FROM **GERMANY!**

Germany is a young country. Until about 120 years ago most Germans lived in small states. Germany only came into existence in 1871. The country was split again, into East and West Germany, from 1945 to 1990.

Because the Germans have only shared the same country for a short time, they have many festivals from different areas. Some of them are much older than the Christian religion Germans follow today.

There are about 78 million Germans. They all speak German. Generally, those in the north speak High German, but there are many local dialects, especially in the south of the country.

**How do you say...**

Hello

**Guten Tag**

Goodbye

**Auf Wiedersehen**

Thank you

**Danke**

Peace

**Friede**

# ADVENT

*The four weeks leading up to Christmas are a time of celebration all over the country as the Germans prepare for the coming holiday.*

Towns all over Germany have special outdoor markets. The stalls sell presents, decorations, and Christmas food. Children buy or make Advent calendars to count the days until Christmas. They also make wreaths of pine branches with four candles. Each Sunday they light one more candle, sing Christmas songs, and eat special cookies.

Children help bake special Advent cakes and cookies. They love *Stollen*, a kind of sweet bread brushed with sugar.

In the first week of Advent, on December 6, children wake up to

*Craftsmen in eastern Germany are famous for their fine woodwork. Traditional figures are favorites as Christmas ornaments.*

*Children enjoy making cookies that symbolize Advent, such as this wreath made of gingerbread.*

find candy and fruit have been left for them by Saint Nicholas, who is like Santa Claus.

In the south of the country Advent is also the time for "knocking nights." Children go from house to house making lots of noise. In return, they are given presents of candy or money.

8

# ADVENT CALENDAR

German children use advent calendars to count down the days until Christmas. There are many different kinds. Some are made out of paper and show a different picture for each day. Others have candy or chocolates. You can make your own advent calendar with individual pockets to hold treats for each day until Christmas.

### YOU WILL NEED
*Different colored felt material*
*Fabric glue*
*Needle and thread*
*Colored yarn*
*A long wooden pole*

**1** Cut a large felt rectangle for the background. For the pockets cut 4 long strips and 2 short ones as shown. Pin the strips, then sew them onto the background to make the pockets. Cut out the numbers and glue them into place.

**2** Cut out your designs and glue them to the calendar. You can follow the patterns shown or you can create your own. Save two small strips of felt and sew them to the top of the calendar as loops. Thread the pole

through. Cut short lengths of yarn for the tassels. Glue them onto either side of the pole.

# THE GOLDEN ANGEL

*The Christmas story is about Mother Mary and her Child. This story is about father love. Baby Jesus and the Golden Angel are found in every German home at Christmas.*

THREE HUNDRED YEARS ago in the city of Nuremberg there lived a craftsman. Everyone agreed that his toyshop was the finest in the city. Every time he finished something, he would add it to the display in his front window. Sometimes children could be seen with their noses pressed against the glass, staring longingly inside.

The craftsman had a little daughter whom he loved more than anything else in the world. He often spent his days making brightly painted wooden toys for his little girl. But he made enough toys to sell so that their lives were comfortable. They had everything they needed. But then his happiness was shattered.

When his daughter was still a child, she got sick and died. The craftsman was overcome with grief. He was too sad to work.

More months passed until it was exactly a year since his daughter's death. That very night the craftsman had a strange dream. His daughter appeared to him as an angel, wearing a high golden head-dress. She had two huge golden wings. The craftsman knew he must carve his little daughter as an angel.

He worked for days. First he carved her face. Then he made a dress and two huge wings, all out of the finest gold leaf. When at last he was finished, he was so tired he fell fast asleep while still sitting at his worktable.

After the shop had been closed for a few days, the craftsman's friends began to worry. They looked through the gaps in his shutters. They saw him asleep in his chair. In front of him on the table was a Golden Angel.

They loved the angel so much they begged the craftsman to make more for presents at Christmas time. He decided that he would carve Golden Angels until he made one that was an exact copy of his dream daughter.

By Christmas he had carved many angels, all beautiful and each slightly different. He sold them all. The next year the same thing happened. And although he never quite equaled the beauty of his dream angel, he found peace and became a rich and busy man.

# CHRISTMAS

*After the long wait through Advent Christmas finally comes. In Germany Christmas Eve is even more important than Christmas Day.*

The idea of a fir tree to mark the season of Christmas started in Germany. Hundreds of years ago people began to decorate these trees with paper flowers, apples, and candy. Later they put little candles on the branches because the flames recalled the star that shone on the night Christ was born. The tree is the heart of ritual on Christmas Eve. All the children go out for the day as their parents decorate the tree in secret. At about six o'clock a bell rings. This is the noisy signal that calls everyone to the living room to see the tree.

This is the first time the children have seen it. The tree is hung with decorations and tinsel and lighted up with candles and sparklers. Some of the little ones think Baby Jesus decorated the Christmas tree.

Beneath the tree is a model of the stable that Jesus was born in. There are also Christmas presents. Now the

*The golden angel is not a religious symbol. She is the heroine of a folk story. Every German child knows the tale, and the angel always has a place on the Christmas tree.*

family exchanges gifts and sings Christmas songs.

Christmas Eve is a family occasion. After all the presents have been opened, Germans stay home where they enjoy a festive meal. They used to eat carp. This is a fish that was favored in the past, when the church did not allow people to eat meat on some days. But nowadays people choose to eat roast goose, turkey, or duck for their Christmas Eve dinner.

*Decorations are made of straw or tinsel. Some are cookies. Models of Baby Jesus also adorn the tree.*

# GINGERBREAD COOKIES

### MAKES 12 TO 14
*1½ cups all-purpose flour*
*1 tsp ground ginger*
*½ tsp baking soda*
*4 tbsp butter or margarine, cut up*
*⅓ cup light brown sugar*
*2 tbsp light corn syrup*
*1 small egg, beaten*
*Store-bought decorations and frosting*

**1** Heat oven to 375°F.
**2** Sift flour, ginger, and baking soda into a bowl. Add butter. Cut in butter until crumbly. Stir in sugar. Make a well in the middle.

**3** Put syrup in a microwave-safe bowl. Microwave on High 15 seconds. Add syrup and egg to well in flour.
**4** Stir until a soft dough forms. Lightly flour countertop. Knead dough on counter until smooth.
**5** Use a lightly floured rolling pin to roll out dough ¼-inch thick. Use a 3-inch cookie cutter to cut cookies. Reroll trimmings. Put cookies on greased cookie sheets.
**6** Bake 10 to 15 minutes until golden. Cool on wire racks.

**7** Attach decorations as shown with drops of frosting.

Following all the excitement, Christmas Day is quiet. But things grow more lively over the Twelve Days of Christmas. Germans once thought that

*This model, made of metal, shows the shepherds visiting Baby Jesus in the stable where he was born.*

the world was full of spirits at this time. In places people still fire

guns at night or beat drums to drive the spirits away.

On January 6 boys dress up to mark the visit of the Three Kings to Jesus. They

# SILENT NIGHT

Stil - le Nacht, hei- li- ge Nacht! Al - les schläft,

ein - sam wacht nur das trau- te, hoch- hei- li- ge Paar.

Hol - der Kna - be im lok- ki- gen Haar, schlaf in himm- li-scher

Ruh! ——— Schlaf —— in himm - li- scher Ruh!

Silent night, holy night,
All is calm, all is bright.
'Round yon virgin mother
and child,
Holy Infant so tender and
mild.
Sleep in heavenly peace,
Sleep in heavenly peace.

carry a star on a pole and sing carols. They chalk doors with the letters K, M, and B for Kaspar, Melchior, and Balthasar, the names of the three kings.

January 6 marks the end of Christmas. The decorations are put away for another year. But the children get to eat the candies left on the tree.

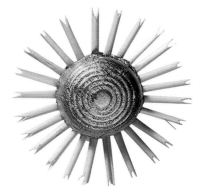

# NEW YEAR

*New Year's Eve in Germany is a noisy time as people follow traditional ways of ensuring good luck for the coming year.*

The shops sell all kinds of special things for the New Year. People buy streamers, squeakers, and firecrackers. They also buy jokes like candy with mustard inside. All these things make for a big party on New Year's Eve.

Friends or families celebrate the New Year with parties and balls. Usually a cold buffet is served, with herring salad or smoked salmon. Church bells ring to signal that midnight has come. Party-goers open champagne and eat a special kind of New Year doughnut. Everyone toasts each other and wishes each other good luck.

Hugs and kisses are exchanged. Then all go outside to greet friends and neighbors. Soon the sky is lighted up as everyone sets off bright fireworks.

The New Year is the time that many people hope for good luck. Chimney sweeps are

*The pig brings luck and money. The chimney sweep, with his broom, clears away bad luck. Devils are chased away, and the New Year starts with high hopes.*

*All these figures of good luck are used to decorate the table at New Year. They can be made in wood or plastic, but these are marzipan versions that bring real pleasure. They can be eaten!*

hard. People have fun reading things into the curious shapes the lead forms. A long and thin shape, for example, might be a boat. That could be a sign that the person who dropped the lead in the water is going on a trip. It might resemble a purse, a sign that the year will be a rich one.

In some parts of Germany brass bands play on top of church towers to greet the New Year. In Bavaria everyone turns out all the lights just before midnight. They turn them on again as the clock strikes twelve.

High up in the Alps everyone tries to make as much noise as they can. They crack their whips and fire their guns and even fire old cannons.

After all the noise and excitement, and parties, New Year's Day can be quiet. Everyone takes the day off work to catch up on their sleep.

thought to be lucky. Certain games are played to predict whether the year will be a lucky one.

One of the most common ways to try to tell the future is by using lead. The lead is heated up until it melts. Then it is dropped into cold water, where it gets

*Hot lead is dropped into cold water. It hardens into unusual shapes, which can be seen as signs. The sign shown here can be interpreted as an owl on a branch. Perhaps this means a wise year ahead.*

# FASCHING

*Carnival is a Christian custom, but rites to mark winter's end and the hungry days before spring are older than the church.*

Fasching, which is the word used for carnival in the German language, is widely celebrated by Catholics. It marks the start of Lent, a time of fasting that recalls the forty days that Jesus spent in the wilderness. Easter, the time that marks the death of Jesus, comes at the end of Lent. For many Christians Fasching is a hearty celebration before the Lenten fast. In pre-Christian days people feasted to finish the winter food supplies, then went hungry until the first spring crops ripened. Today it is a time for everyone to have fun.

All over Germany Fasching has parades, decorated floats, and people dressed up as jesters and clowns. In November committees in many towns across Germany start to plan Fasching. In January the towns elect their Fasching prince. A very famous Fasching celebration takes place in the city of Cologne. The carnival has been held in the city for over 150 years.

The highpoint of Fasching comes in the week before Lent. On the Thursday women dress up and take power in the city. This began as a protest that Fasching was once only for men.

The next Monday, called Rose Monday, sees a big parade. The line of floats, clowns,

*People used to believe that masks frightened evil spirits. Now it has become part of the fun to wear these ugly faces at Fasching parades.*

and bands stretches five miles long. More than a million people come to watch. The people taking part in the parade throw gifts of candy and flowers into the excited, watching crowd.

*Witch figures are common at Fasching. They recall the old beliefs when country people used to feel that the dark nights of winter were full of strange spirits.*

# FRIED RING DOUGHNUTS

### MAKES 12
*1½ cups all-purpose flour*
*½ tsp baking powder*
*Pinch of salt*
*⅔ cup milk, warm*
*4 tbsp butter, melted*
*2 large eggs, beaten*
*4 tbsp sugar*
*Vegetable oil*
*for deep-frying*

**1** You will need an adult to help you fry the doughnuts. Sift flour, baking powder, and salt into a mixing bowl.

**2** In another bowl mix butter, half the eggs, and sugar.

**3** Make a well in middle of the flour. Pour in egg mixture. Stir, gradually incorporating flour. Stir in warm milk to make a smooth, soft dough.

**4** Divide dough into 12 pieces. Using lightly floured hands, roll each piece into a 3-inch rope.

**5** Shape each dough rope into a ring. Use remaining beaten egg to seal ends together.

**6** Ask an adult to deep-fry a few doughnuts at a time in vegetable oil at 350°F. Drain each doughnut well on paper towels and sprinkle with sugar.

# EASTER

*As in many other Christian countries, the Germans celebrate Easter with eggs and other signs that spring has come.*

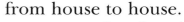

Christians mark the death and resurrection of Christ at Easter.

In Germany the holiday starts on Good Friday, the day on which Christ died. The day is also known as "Quiet Friday." This is because it is a time of sadness. In Catholic churches no bells are rung. Instead people make wooden rattles that clatter when they are spun. They use the rattles instead of bells to call people to church.

On the next day, Saturday, the children light huge bonfires. These are made of wood and rubbish they collect by going from house to house.

Easter Sunday is the day that Jesus is believed to have risen from the dead. Many villages hold an Easter walk or ride in memory of the walk that

*Christians believe that on the third day after He was crucified, Christ rose from the dead. Eggs and baby chicks are symbols of new life, and pictures of them are popular on Easter decorations.*

*There is an old German story about the hare school and some naughty hare pupils. At Easter children display models of the teacher, his board, and his class of young spring hares.*

Christ took with His disciples after His resurrection. In one of these processions a man dressed as Saint George rides on a white horse. In another, men on horseback gallop past a post shaped like a cross. The winner is presented with a cake shaped like a horse,

## ALMOND-PASTE EGGS

**MAKES 30**
*8 ounces almond paste
Red, yellow, and green edible
food colors
Confectioners' sugar*

**1** Divide almond paste into 3 equal pieces. Place each piece in a separate bowl.

**2** Add 10 to 15 drops red food coloring to one bowl. Use your hands to work in coloring until almond paste is solid color.

**3** Wash your hands. Repeat to make yellow and green almond paste.

**4** Break each color almond paste into 10 equal pieces. Roll into small egg shapes in the sugar. Chill until ready to eat.

21

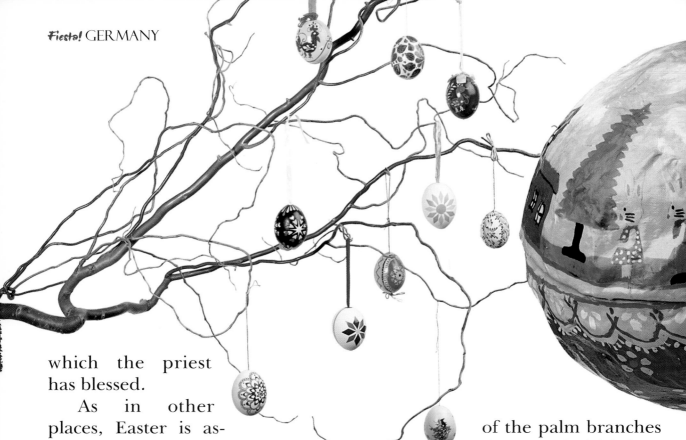

which the priest has blessed.

As in other places, Easter is associated with signs of spring and new life. The most common are eggs. On Easter Sunday children hunt for eggs in the garden. They are made of chocolate or candy, or are decorated hens' eggs. The eggs are left in little nests, which are like baskets lined with strips of green paper like grass.

Some children are told that the eggs are left by the Easter hare, who brings them in a

*All over Europe country people always painted hens' eggs for the Easter festivities. They emptied the eggs or hardboiled them before they decorated the shells.*

small wheelbarrow. They can buy models of the hare made of chocolate. In other areas the eggs are left by a rooster or a fox.

At home eggs are hung on twigs. Other decorations are willow or hazel branches, which are a reminder

of the palm branches that people laid down for Christ's donkey to walk on as He rode into Jerusalem before the crucifixion.

Apart from Easter eggs, one of the most common Easter foods is bread. Sometimes it is baked in the shape of a lamb, another animal associated with the spring. Another kind of bread comes in the shape of a man holding an egg. The egg cooks at the same time as the bread.

# PAPIER-MÂCHÉ EGGS

Eggs are found in every home at Easter. People give each other presents of chocolate or candy eggs. Some gift eggs are made of china or silver and gold! But handmade gifts, like this papier-mâché egg, are the best of all.

This egg is made in two sections. One half becomes the lid. Pack the lower half with straw or tissue paper or cotton balls. Hide marzipan eggs, or chocolate ones, in this soft bedding. Decorate the shell with pictures of spring blossoms or chicks, or copy the hares going to school shown here.

## YOU WILL NEED
*A balloon*
*Newspaper and cardboard*
*Wallpaper paste*
*Poster paints*
*Quick-dry acrylic varnish*

**1** Blow up balloon to the size and shape of a very large egg. Cover the balloon with long strips of newspaper, attaching them with wallpaper paste. Tie a string to the knot of the balloon and hang to dry. Draw a clear line around the balloon as shown. Cut the papier-mâché sphere along the line with scissors.

**2** Set aside one of the halves of the sphere for the lid of the egg. Cover the cut edge with small strips of newspaper and wallpaper paste. Allow to dry. For the bottom of the egg cut two cardboard strips the length of the circumference of the egg. One strip should be 1/2 inch wide and the other 1 inch wide.

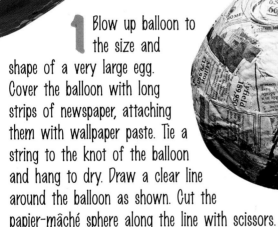

**3** Take the 1/2-inch wide strip and glue it to the inside rim of the egg. Fit and glue the 1 inch strip into 1/2-inch strip. The two strips should line up at the bottom, but not at the top. The 1 inch strip stands higher. Cover the strips with newspaper and newspaper paste and let dry. Paint both sides with white. Now paint on your design. Apply a coat of varnish to give a nice finish.

# MAY DAY

**Although May 1 is Labor Day in Germany and a public holiday, it is also a time when people observe many much older traditions.**

In the countryside May Day is the time for following old customs. Many are based on the May Pole. This is a tall tree, usually a fir, which is cut down, stripped of all but its top branches, and decorated with ribbons. It is put up in the center of the village or town. The pole is brought in from the forest by groups of young men, who all wear identical caps. The towns and villages compete to see which can have the tallest May Pole.

The top of the May Pole is crowned with a May wreath of branches. The wreath is often hung with sausages or candy. These are rewards for any young people who manage to climb to the top of the pole.

Once the pole is put up, it becomes the focus of the village's May Day celebrations. People gather around it to dance or to drink, and in the past sports

*Traditionally, spring was a time when the young chose marriage partners. A May Pole dance was a chance to meet your true love.*

events were organized for the young men.

Many old May Day rituals concern love. Young men used to make small models of May Poles out of birch twigs. They would hang or plant them outside the home of the girl they loved.

A ceremony held every three years in the Bavarian town of Antdorf also concerns girls and boys. The boys sit on a bench, holding a lantern and two brooms. The girls, of whom there are three fewer than there are boys, creep up behind them. They tip over the bench, and all grab the hand of a boy. The three boys who are left out have to dance with the lantern and brooms.

In other areas May Day is celebrated by groups of young men. In one town apprentices parade in peaked caps and blue and white sashes. In the city of Heidelberg students sing through the night of April 30 to welcome the arrival of May. In other towns brass bands greet the early dawn.

*Country skills are still admired. On certain occasions even city folk put on traditional clothes, such as this hunter wears. This May Pole carries plants and animals celebrating the importance of farmers and country life.*

# SAINT MARTIN'S DAY

*Saint Martin's Day marks the end of the harvest and the coming of the long, cold German winter.*

On November 11 the German people mark the coming of winter on Saint Martin's Day. In many ways the celebration is like a harvest festival in other countries. All the grain, fruit, and grapes are stored, ready for the winter.

Saint Martin was a bishop who lived a long time ago. He used to be the patron saint of all shepherds, and his feast day was a holiday for them. On this day they would summon their lords by blowing on their horns. They would give them presents of decorated branches. Then they bargained for better contracts and more pay for the coming year.

Germans used to eat goose on this day. This was because a story told how Martin once hid in a flock of

geese when people were trying to make him a bishop. He did not think he was holy enough for the job. But the geese cackled and gave him away, so Saint Martin became a bishop after all.

Another special food is bread in the shape of a man with a clay pipe. This is given to children on Saint Martin's Day.

It is a busy day for German children. At dusk they parade through the streets with paper lanterns they have bought or made. Sometimes a band plays too. The bright lanterns come in many shapes and sizes, but most are in the form of the sun or the moon and the stars.

Sometimes, mainly in Catholic areas, the children sing songs to Saint Martin as they parade along the streets. Protestants do not believe in saints, so in Protestant areas children sing songs about their lanterns, the sun, and the moon.

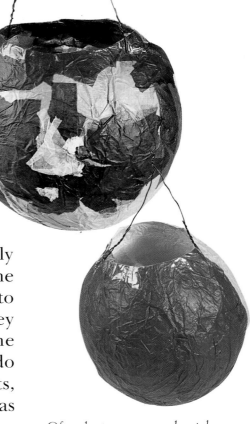

*Often lanterns are made at home from papier-mâché. Store-bought lanterns are made from paper.*

# LATERNE, LATERNE

Later ne, La - ter - ne, Son - ne, Mond und Ster - ne, bren - ne auf, mein Licht, bren - ne auf, mein Licht, a - ber nur mei - ne lie - be La - ter - ne nicht. ter - ne nicht.

Lantern, lantern
Sun, moon and stars
Burn up my light
Burn up my light
But don't burn my dear
Lantern.

27

# THE LIFE OF SAINT MARTIN

*Saint Martin was born around 316. The Roman Empire ruled most of Europe. However, barbarians, people from outside the Empire, were fighting the Roman army. Martin was a loyal Roman soldier until Jesus visited him in a dream.*

A column of Roman soldiers was riding across the plains of northern France. It was a bitter, cold winter's day. They were exhausted. "Not far now," shouted the soldiers' leader, Martin. The men could see their destination, the town of Amiens, in the distance.

Amiens was being threatened by the barbarians who lived beyond the borders of the Roman Empire. Tomorrow there would be a battle. Many of the soldiers were wondering whether they would live to see their families again. Martin had shouted words of encouragement all day. Martin always tried to act in a Christian way, although his parents worshipped the old Roman gods. For hundreds of years Christianity had been forbidden. The Roman rulers used to throw Christians to the lions to be eaten. But in 313, only three years before Martin was born, the Roman emperor Constantine I became a Christian himself. Martin, too, had chosen the new faith.

At last the soldiers reached the gates of the town. As they were going through, Martin looked down and saw a beggar wearing very little and shivering in the cold. Martin stopped.

St. Martin.

His troop of fellow soldiers galloped toward the town center. Martin did not move. What did he have to give the hungry man? He had no money or food to offer. But the soldier did have something to share. He cut his thick cloak in two and gave one half to the poor, sad beggar.

That night Jesus appeared to Martin in a dream and told him that he, Christ, had been that shivering beggar. Martin knew then that he must give his life to God. The next day Martin asked his officer if he could leave the army. "I can no longer be a Roman soldier," he said. "I must devote myself to Jesus."

Martin lived a holy life, first as a humble monk and then, later, as a bishop. He was greatly loved for his goodness, and after he died in 397, he was made a saint.

# DRIVING DOWN THE CATTLE

*At the end of the summer German farmers move their cattle from the mountain pastures for the winter.*

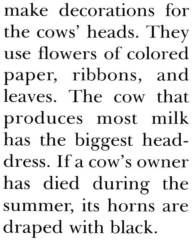

In the Alpine south of Germany cattle spend the summer in the high mountain pastures. When the weather grows worse, early in October, the farmers lead them back down to the villages in lively parades.

For days before the journey starts, the cowherds make decorations for the cows' heads. They use flowers of colored paper, ribbons, and leaves. The cow that produces most milk has the biggest head-dress. If a cow's owner has died during the summer, its horns are draped with black.

On the day of the journey everyone puts on their best clothes, and the procession begins. It is usually led by a young milk-maid or cowherd.

The cows all wear big bells under their necks that ring as they

*The milkmaids and their cow are cut from thin metal. The color is enameled on the surface. The figure of the cow shows her flower wreath, a sign of her importance to farmers. The grand procession of animals is a way of honoring their role in providing food and milk.*

walk. Everyone can hear them coming. By the time they reach the village, everyone is there to cheer them.

Everyone is happy that the cows are safe for the winter. In most places the villagers celebrate the day with a special meal.

# WORDS TO KNOW

**Advent:** The period beginning four Sundays before Christmas.

**Alpine:** Mountainous, or actually in the Alps. The Alps are a mountain range that stretches from southern Germany to northern Italy

**Altar:** A table on which worshipers leave offerings, burn incense, or perform ceremonies.

**Apprentice:** A young person who is being taught the skills of his or her job by a master craftsman.

**Contract:** An agreement between two people in which each one promises to do something for the other.

**Dialect:** A regional variety of a language.

**Empire:** A group of countries ruled by an emperor or an empress.

**Minister:** A person who conducts Protestant church services.

**Patron saint:** A saint who watches over a particular group. Nations, towns, and professions all have patron saints.

**Protestant:** A member of one of the Protestant churches, which together form one of the three main branches of Christianity. The Protestants split from the Roman Catholic Church in the sixteenth century.

**Resurrection:** The rising of Christ from the dead on Easter Sunday.

**Roman Catholic:** A member of the Roman Catholic Church, the largest branch of Christianity. The head of this church is the pope.

**Saint:** A title given to very holy people by some Christian churches. Saints are important in the Roman Catholic Church.

**Sash:** A band worn around the waist or over one shoulder.

**Scholar:** A person of great learning.

## ACKNOWLEDGMENTS

### WITH THANKS TO:

Bayerischer Kunstgewerbe-Verein c.v., Munich Nativity p14-15, Easter artefacts p20-21, Maypole figures p24-25, dairy artefacts p30. Dagmar Plocher papier-mâché lanterns p29. B.Schätz, angel p12, mask, witch p18-19, hare school p20-21.

### PHOTOGRAPHS BY:

All photographs by Bruce Mackie.
Cover photograph by Pictor International.

### ILLUSTRATIONS BY:

Fiona Saunders title page, p4-5, Mountain High Maps ® Copyright © 1993 Digital Wisdom, Inc. p4-5. Tracy Rich p7. Alison Fleming p10.

# SET CONTENTS